More Than Conquerors

The following reflections were originally printed as single units:

SPIRITUAL QUICKSAND
RIVERS OF WATERS
PERFECTED PRAISE

Reprinted by permission
NAZARENE PUBLISHING HOUSE

WHY JESUS HELD HIS PEACE

Used by permission
Copyright 1968 by *ETERNITY*

Scripture quotations are from the KING JAMES VERSION of the Bible, with the following exceptions:

WASTE

Taken from *The Modern Language Bible, The New Berkeley Version in Modern English,* ©1959, 1969 by Zondervan Publishing House
Used by permission

HE'S ONLY THE CARPENTER, MARY'S SON

From the *Revised Standard Version of the Bible*
Copyrighted 1946, 1952© 1971, 1973

4

More Than Conquerors

Reflections in Psalm 119:133-176

by
Virginia Corfield

The Provident Press
P. O. Box 1112
Covina, CA 91722

THE REFLECTION SERIES . . .
books that mirror the Word of God.

THE DISCOVERY ROOM
AT LIBERTY
A CELESTIAL FIX
MORE THAN CONQUERORS

OTHER BOOKS BY VIRGINIA CORFIELD . . .

SOW THE WIND
REAP THE WHIRLWIND

IN LOVING MEMORY OF
DOUGLAS PARSONS
1947-1968
More Than a Conqueror

A PERSONAL NOTE

The years I have lived in Psalm 119 have been the most rewarding I have ever known. As each day passes, I am more than ever convinced that all truth is to be found in its precepts; all fulness of life, all joy. I cannot imagine life without it.

The reflections in this book are but responses, brief "Thank You" notes to the Lord for this magnificent portion of His Word. In themselves, they are flawed and very human — mere figures of the true. But if *as you read them* the Holy Spirit deals with you as He has with me, they will serve you well.

Virginia Corfield

THE PSALM OF PSALMS

Over the centuries, Bible scholars have extolled the wonderful words of Psalm 119. Even today, as men consider the breathtaking magnitude of its design, they are awestricken.

THE PSALM OF PSALMS!

Truly, this psalm is a literary masterpiece. A flawless acrostic some have fondly called, "A Saint's Alphabet."

It is divided into twenty-two sections, according to the number of letters of the Hebrew alphabet, with each section consisting of eight verses. Thus the first eight verses all begin with "Aleph" in the original, the second eight with "Beth," and so on . . .

Through one hundred and seventy-six verses.

Think of it! One hundred and seventy-six different ways of saying "How love I thy law"!

It is an amazing *tour de force.*

Moreover, it is an appropriate framework for its lofty theme, for by its words the *language of earth* is used to magnify *the language of heaven.*

That is, the Word of God.

MORE THAN CONQUERORS focuses upon five and one-half sections of this monumental psalm: Pe (one-half), Tzaddi, Koph, Resh, Schin and Tau. It covers verses one hundred and thirty-three through one hundred and seventy-six.

PE

צ

TZADDI

ק

KOPH

ר

RESH

ש

SCHIN

ת

TAU

פ

PE

Psalm 119:133-136

The Attraction of Sin
Social Security
A Climate of Love
Rivers of Waters

THE ATTRACTION OF SIN

"Order my steps in thy word: and let not any iniquity have dominion over me" (Psalm 119:133).

Man has much to learn about the heavens. Every discovery he makes opens new vistas to be explored. Every answer he finds leads to further questions.

Yet for all this, certain fundamental laws have been established. Of these, one of the most obvious is this: *Lunar gravity* is a force to be reckoned with.

Now the same could be said of *the attraction of sin!*

For just as the invisible bonds of lunar gravity draw a spacecraft close to the moon, so the gravitational pull of the forces of Satan attract a man to iniquity.

And as the unseen forces of the moon have power to tether a craft in lunar orbit, so the satanic powers of darkness hook a man in compulsive patterns of sin.

Unfortunately, this is a basic truth man seldom reckons with when he begins "to enjoy the pleasures of sin *for a season.*"

Such an oversight is not surprising, of course, for man's low scanning orbit over the rocky terrain of the Sea of Nector and the Sea of Fertility is frequently without incident. And so is his descent to the Sea of Tranquility.

But just let him try to ascend!

Before long, he finds that *in himself* he has no power to overcome the tug of sin's attraction. His slow burn of shame cannot provide sufficient thrust to break him free of satanic domination.

Inevitably, he is drawn back against his will. Recaptured. Pinned in an orbit of slow death . . .

Or dashed to destruction.

Then is there no hope? No way of escape?
Is there no way of attaining escape velocity?

There is! The law of the Spirit of Life in Christ Jesus!

For the propulsive resurrection power that raised Christ from the dead can free any man from Satan's sphere of influence . . .

If only he will yield to the Spirit's control!

SOCIAL SECURITY

"Deliver me from the oppression of man: so will I keep thy precepts" (Psalm 119:134).

Jesus knew what He was, and why . . .

He was content with the identity God had given Him, pleased with the plan of God for His life and secure in the love of God.

Consequently, even on the cross He was free: free to act rather than react, free to think of others rather than self . . .

Free to give love rather than seek it.

In a sense, this remarkable freedom to be Himself *regardless of others* was not surprising. Throughout His incarnation, Jesus displayed a divine sense of self-hood in His relationships.

As a young boy, He was neither overawed by the doctors in the Temple, nor overpossessed by His anxious mother. He was respectful, but not reverent. Submissive, but not subjugated.

In His public ministry, He moved with equal poise among people of all kinds: great and small, godly and ungodly. He was at ease with others because He was at ease with Himself. He was secure socially because He rested in the self-concept He received from His Father God . . .

Not in the image of Himself He found reflected in man.

Thus when He came to His own and His own received Him not, He was able to go on . . .

And when the common people heard Him gladly and wanted to make Him king, He was able to walk away.

He was free at all times. Singularly free from oppression in the inner man. No matter what opinion people held of him, He did not change. He was always Himself. He played no roles.

Nor did He allow people to stamp Him with a preconceived image, squeeze Him into another mold or manipulate Him like a puppet on a string.

He was meek, *but not weak.* Humble, *but not lacking in self-respect.* Lowly, *but not a doormat.*

He knew what was in man . . . and in Himself.

O that we who are *in Christ* would be as content with the identity God has given us: *accepted in the Beloved.*

Then we would be delivered from the oppressive sovereignty of man's approval or disapproval. And we also would be free.

Free to act rather than react, free to think of others rather than self . . .

Free to give love rather than seek it.

A CLIMATE OF LOVE

"Make thy face to shine upon thy servant; and teach me thy statutes" (Psalm 119:135).

Tommy smiled shyly and slipped a test paper into his mother's outstretched hand. As her eyes skimmed over the page, she shook her head in amazement.

"Tommy, another good grade! What's happened to you? You always used to have a great deal of trouble with math. But now you seem to understand it so well! What's the secret of your success, young man?"

"Well, Mom, I sort of . . . well, ya see . . ."

All at once, Tommy's face was radiant!

"It's my teacher, Mom! When I can't seem to think on a test, I just look up and there she is standing by me, smiling at me! And Mom, I feel so good inside . . .

"I could do anything!"

Whenever there is a loving relationship between the teacher and the one being taught, there will be *a climate of love* and a rich harvest of learning.

For as the warmth of the sun brings forth an abundant crop from the earth, so the sunshine of a smile encourages growth in a human heart.

When one knows he is loved, the soil of his heart is ready for the seed of learning.

And when one belongs to Jesus, he is truly blessed in all the problems of life.

For our Lord is not a Harsh Taskmaster who demands, but a Good Teacher who always stands by . . .

Smiling, encouraging, supporting.

It is His responsibility to see that we are equipped to pass life's tests. Our part is simply to trust and obey . . .

And look up to Him:
   "Make thy face to shine upon thy servant;
      and teach me thy statutes."

And as we behold and reflect His glory, we will be changed into His likeness . . .

For He teaches His lessons face-to-face

In a heartwarming climate of love.

RIVERS OF WATERS

"Rivers of waters run down mine eyes, because they keep not thy law" (Psalm 119:136).

It was only a "routine" church visit in the home . . .

Lovingly, Marge looked at Betty, the mother of a girl in her Sunday School class. She asked an innocent question: "Is your daughter interested in spiritual things?"

Without warning, Betty began to sob. Up from the depths of her broken heart gushed torrents of grief, guilt and regrets. She herself had known the way of salvation as a girl, but ignored the voice of the Spirit. There had been poor decisions, broken commandments, hopelessly snarled relationships.

As Betty spoke, the tears in Marge's eyes spilled over. She found herself speaking softly, "Betty, you know that Jesus died for your sins . . . that He is able to save you and bring you to God?"

"Yes . . ."

"Betty, will you receive Him just now as your Saviour? It's not too late."

There was a pause. A painful, drawn out silence.

As she struggled with the Spirit, Betty's face contorted with agony . . . then suddenly became masked! Unsearchable.

Cold, measured words spelled out her answer. "No, I'm not ready." Marge knew she dare not press further. The conversation was over.

Another silence . . .

"Betty, may I pray for you and your family before I leave?"

Marge reached over to Betty, took her hands in her own, and prayed haltingly. She wondered, *What do I do now?*

As she left, the Holy Spirit showed her. Impulsively, she drew Betty into her arms and kissed her.

"I love you, Betty . . ."

The years passed. The barrier and the burden continued.

Then late one night Betty called Marge on the telephone. She got straight to the point. "I'm going to the hospital tomorrow for a serious operation. I'm not ready to go. *I need Jesus!*

"I know you love me . . . will you help me?"

Sometimes even the blessed Holy Spirit needs our help in translating the word "love" into flesh and blood; in bringing into the reality of this world the compassionate heart of Christ — the all-embracing love of the One who wept for the sinners of His own generation.

When we look at those who "keep not thy law," do we see the lostness of their souls without Christ?

Do the "rivers of waters" run down our eyes?

צ

TZADDI

Psalm 119:137-144

Undergirded By Righteousness
"It's Just Like The Book Says!"
Waste
The Pollutions Of The World
Spiritual Quicksand
An Everlasting Righteousness
Your Option For Joy
The Game Of Life

UNDERGIRDED BY RIGHTEOUSNESS

"Righteous art thou, O LORD, and upright are thy judgments" (Psalm 119:137).

When Molly was a little girl, she loved her Bible . . . the pretty pictures, the fine pages edged with gold, the soft imitation-leather cover.
She loved to hold it, to feel it . . .
To bend it at will.

When Molly was older, she loved her Bible even more . . . the beautiful word-portraits of Jesus, the fine-line truths overlaid with gold, the gracious grain of merciful kindness.
She loved to hold the Bible in her heart, to feel it . . .
To bend it at will.

"I like to think of Jesus as . . . In my experience . . . It seems to me . . . I interpret this to mean . . . I feel that . . .
"I cannot believe God would . . . ."

But one day God not only *would*, but *did!*

And under stress, Molly's faulty do-it-yourself theo-

logical framework suddenly gave way . . .
Reducing her impressively structured faith to rubble.

It is true that faith is faith. And yet . . .

It is also true that any faith that is supported by our own prefabricated opinions is doomed to disaster. It may be a beautiful faith . . . fine-line, gracious, sincere. It may be a great faith. Monumental in design.

But for all its strengths, *if it is not built upon the rigidly righteous Word of God,* it is like a house of cards . . .
Insubstantial, subject to imminent collapse.

On the other hand, any faith that rests for support on the upright judgments of God is sure to withstand great stress. In itself, it may not be a high-rise faith. It may even be immature, awkward, sprawling.

But for all its weaknesses, if it so much as lies prone and outstretched on the strong planks of God's promises, it will be enough . . .

For it will be *undergirded* by the righteousness of God.

"IT'S JUST LIKE THE BOOK SAYS!"

"Thy testimonies that thou hast commanded are righteous and very faithful" (Psalm 119:138).

It was late afternoon. A fine mist lightly veiled the rain-washed air. In the west, the sun lay low on the horizon; in the east, a brilliantly hued bow arched heavenward.

Danny raced out the front door, science book in hand.

For a moment, he stopped to stare at the sight before him. Then he lowered his eyes, opened the book and thumbed rapidly through its pages.

He soon found his place: RAINBOW: REFLECTION AND REFRACTION OF THE SUN'S RAYS AS THEY FALL ON DROPS OF RAIN; BANDS OF VIOLET, INDIGO, BLUE, GREEN, YELLOW, ORANGE, RED.

Keeping his finger on the text, he looked up to check for himself. VIOLET, INDIGO, BLUE, GREEN, YELLOW, ORANGE, RED.

He paused. Awestricken.

"Well, what do you know?
"It's just like the book says!"

O that on days when the sun lays low on the horizon of our hopes, we would shift our gaze from our shadowed feelings to that which we know *by faith*.

Then in life's tear-drenched hours, when we see nothing ahead but a misty veil of confusion, we would be able to stand fast, find our place in God's Book, and look up to see His *bow of faithfulness* arching over us . . .

Reflecting rays of tender-mercies, compassions, grace.

For as the rainbow is the token of God's covenant with every living creature, so the testimonies are the mark of His everlasting agreement with all who come to Him through Christ.

Both are fixed in His righteousness. Therefore, both are immutable. Inviolate. Even God Himself can never change their heavenly order, for He abides faithful . . .

And He cannot deny Himself.

So in spite of our variable feelings, clouded vision and overcast souls, the forecast for today reads:
CONTINUED FAITHFULNESS.

And to lift Danny's words:
"It's just like the Book says!"

WASTE

"My zeal hath consumed me, because mine enemies have forgotten thy words" (Psalm 119:139).

While at Bethany in the house of Simon the leper, Jesus was reclining at the table, when a woman came with an alabaster jar of pure nard perfume, very valuable and, breaking the jar, she poured the ointment on His head.

But there were some who indignantly remarked to one another, "What use is this waste of ointment?"

But Jesus said, "Leave her alone! She has treated Me nobly.
"She has done what she could."

As we look at this woman through the eyes of Christ, we begin to fathom the depths of devotion that welled within her soul.

We sense the adoration that could not be contained within the narrow confines of religious ritual, but must burst forth in an overflowing expression of love.

We see the consuming zeal that compelled her to seek to symbolize His approaching death in a tangible way.

A way few understood . . .

For the disciples, having forgotten His words, saw only the outward appearance of her act: the irretrievable ointment poured forth without measure, the jar broken beyond repair, the great cost.
"What use is this waste?"

It is possible that at some time we have been filled with ardor to translate the beauty of our Saviour into earthly terms. At a given moment in time we have experienced an overflowing of love; a surging of desire to respond to His cross in a personal way.

With the vision of His sacrifice before us, we have broken open the jar of all that is dear to us with sweeping decisions, lavish acts of obedience and extravagant devotion.

And now, our hearts shattered by the unforseen effects of our fervent zeal as it spilled over into the lives of others . . .

We see only the great cost.

And we also question:
"What use is this waste?"

Then we look long at the cross of our Lord . . .
And know the answer.

THE POLLUTIONS OF THE WORLD

"Thy word is very pure: therefore thy servant loveth it"
(Psalm 119:140).

From the day Adam rebelled against God and acquired an old sin nature, man has evidenced a fantastic ability for polluting his world.

Out of his heart proceed evil thoughts, murders, adulteries, fornications, thefts, false witness, blasphemies . . .

And out of his mouth spew deadly poisons.

He blows his stack . . . and up from the blast-furnace wastes within his soul rise sulfurous compounds of anger and wrath. With every belching emission, toxic clouds of bitterness billow into the air, heavy-hanging layers of resentments suspend in the atmosphere and eye-stinging judgments cast a disagreeable pall.

He gushes . . . and out of his inner wild wells of iniquity spurt all manner of obscenities, expletives and crude defilements that befoul the mainstream of life.

"Unclean! Unclean!" cries the man whose hope is in the Lord; the man who longs to be pure, *even as Christ is pure.*

But where can he go to escape the pollutions of the world?

A monastery, an ivory tower, a South Seas island — none of these provide the answer. For even if it were possible for him to live in a plastic enclosure of perfect environment . . .

His own pollutions would play havoc with his soul.

No. The answer to the believer's pollution problem is to be found in the Word of God.

In the *daily washing* of the "water of the Word."

For the Word itself is pure. So pure it is totally impervious to the infiltration of evil. It is not defiled, adulterated or contaminated in any way.

Consequently, when a man *daily exposes every facet of his soul to the pure thoughts of God,* a purification process is effected within him. Worldly impurities, foreign particles and extraneous matters are gently lifted and flushed away before they become lodged in his thought patterns . . .

And he is able to enjoy fellowship with a pure and Holy God.

SPIRITUAL QUICKSAND

"I am small and despised: yet do not I forget thy precepts" (Psalm 119:141).

When we are despised . . .

There is an obvious danger to which we are exposed: that of yielding to the temptation to despise in return. To defend ourselves by rejecting the other person in some way. To tear him down outwardly. Or in our hearts.

That is bad enough. But there is another danger that is even more deadly, because it is more subtle! More deceiving, because it comes disguised as humility. More destructive, because it spirals into despair!

This is the danger of going to the other extreme, and of accepting the contempt of others as a true indication of our "worthlessness" . . .

Of looking beyond the Word of God and His grace
And despising ourselves.

Turning on ourselves because we do not measure up to the standards of other Christians, or fall short of our own desired perfection!

Assuming that because our witness is not being effective, we are an embarrassment to Christ.

Hating ourselves for our mistakes and failures, pouring contempt upon our stumbling efforts, our inabilities.

Joining others in esteeming ourselves as of no value — worthy only to be despised!

Is this godly humility?
Or is this a pit of spiritual quicksand designed by Satan to suck us down into despondency?

When we are overwhelmed by our unworthiness, let us look to Calvary, where Jesus "endured the cross, despising the shame . . ." so that we need not be condemned.
Even by ourselves.

We have no right to despise ourselves . . .
For, as believers in Christ, we have been *accepted in the Beloved.* And we must learn to accept ourselves as God does.
As imperfect human beings. As faulty creatures . . .
Saved by grace.

And if we would doubt our worth, let us remember the price with which we have been bought . . . the blood of Christ.

How shall we despise what is so precious to God?

AN EVERLASTING RIGHTEOUSNESS

"Thy righteousness is an everlasting righteousness, and thy law is the truth" (Psalm 119:142).

The child died.

It was not that he was wicked, for he was not. It was not that God was displeased with him, for He was not.

On the contrary, it was because there was found in him something good and pleasing, *"some good thing toward the LORD God of Israel,"* that he died.

At such a revelation, the man who deems himself more just than God explodes with self-righteous indignation. "How could a loving God take the life of an innocent child?

"God is unrighteous, unfair and unjust!"

But let the man who so maligns God consider this:

Before the foundation of the world, the righteousness of God planned for the child's salvation. On the cross, the love of God bore his sins that he could be cleansed of all unrighteousness.

During his brief life span on earth, the child responded to the light given: believing God, trusting in Him, obeying Him as best he could.

At his death, he was delivered from the power of darkness, and translated into the kingdom of God's dear Son . . .

To live with Him forever.

So let no one be deceived. The righteousness of God is an everlasting righteousness. Absolute. Inviolate. Eternal in the heavens. It is not subject to man's interpretation, nor does it tremble before his ignorant babblings.

Above all, it is not blind.

For the Lord knows those who are turned toward Him, whether in Israel, *or in Samaria*, or in the uttermost part of the earth.

Day by day, His eyes run to and fro throughout the whole earth, to show Himself strong in behalf of those who stretch out in His direction: searching for light, hungering to know Him. To worship Him in truth.

To such as these, the invisible things of Him from the creation of the world are clearly seen, even His eternal power and Godhead.

In such as these, His righteousness is revealed.

Even in such innocents as Abijah, in whom was found something good and pleasing toward the LORD God of Israel.

Abijah, who was born into God-forsaking heathenism, nourished on molten images and weaned on idolatry. For his father was that wicked King Jeroboam I *"who made Israel to sin" for generations to come.*

And had the child lived, and followed in his father's footsteps . . .

(I Kings 14:1-18)

YOUR OPTION FOR JOY

"Trouble and anguish have taken hold on me: yet thy commandments are my delights" (Psalm 119:143).

Are you picking up your option for joy?

Are you enjoying the delights the commandments of God offer during times of trouble and anguish?

Or are you going through life the hard way . . . Knowing trouble and anguish *only*?

When the Psalmist said, "Trouble and anguish have taken hold on me," he spoke from experience. Surely, there is no absence of tribulation in his life.

Enemies are ever with him
Affliction and suffering meet him in the way
Disappointment and discouragement dog his every step.

He knows heaviness of soul, weariness of mind and numbness of spirit because trouble and anguish *have taken hold on him.*

Yet for all this . . .

He also knows great peace, fervent hope and sheer delight . . . *because he has taken hold on the Word of God.*

He has reached out by choice . . .
And picked up his option for joy.

Have you?

THE GAME OF LIFE

"The righteousness of thy testimonies is everlasting: give me understanding, and I shall live" (Psalm 119:144).

Mary Jo looked at her young daughter out of the corner of her eye. What was she trying to do now?

Patty lay sprawled on the floor, totally absorbed in a new game. A playing board, tokens and miscellaneous pieces of playing equipment were scattered helter-skelter on the rug.

Suddenly Patty moved one of the little "men" from one space to another. Then she shook her head angrily and slammed the board shut.

Mary Jo couldn't hold in any longer. "Honey, why don't you read the rule book so you'll know how to play the game?"

"Oh, Mother," Patty said in a pained tone of voice. "Mother, I'd rather figure it out for myself. I want to see *what I can do first* . . .

"Then if I get stuck, I'll read the rule book!"

How typical Patty is of many of us, and the way we try to play THE GAME OF LIFE! The words, "Please God, I'd rather figure it out for myself," may not actually pass our lips, but they are often the unspoken theme of our hearts.

So like a child who has a new game he doesn't understand, we tend to spread life out before us, make up our own rules, move our little "men" back-and-forth and become hopelessly stuck in a heartbreaking situation . . .

Before we turn to the Rule Book for help.

What a tragedy this is!

For unlike the games children play, THE GAME OF LIFE is real. *Every move we make counts!* We cannot close up the board when we feel frustrated, nor can we go back to "go" and blithely start again.

O Lord . . .
The righteousness of thy testimonies is everlasting: give me understanding, and I shall live."

ק

KOPH

Psalm 119:145-152

Stand-By Prayer
The Friend Of The Downcast
A Mere Tendril Of Faith
Counting Thoughts
An Audience With God
More Than A Conqueror
Even Though
Founded Forever

STAND-BY PRAYER

"I cried with my whole heart; hear me, O LORD: I will keep thy statutes" (Psalm 119:145).

Marion crumpled the letter in her hand.

She moved her lips to pray, but nothing happened. She groped in her mind for words, but there were none.

A feeling of helplessness seized her. What hope had she of reaching God?

She was mute. *Inside and out!*

At one time or another, most of us also come to a place where we cannot pray for ourselves, or anyone else.

With some, this infirmity in prayer is but a small matter. A momentary power failure. Temporary and soon restored.

But with others, it may assume a more serious nature. There may be extended or recurring periods of hysteria, disassociation or mental illness where the mind is not lucid. When this is the case, we will find ourselves unable to pray at all: *for prayer is formed first in the mind* with mental concepts and vocabulary.

What then? If we cannot pray because our thought patterns are incoherent, what hope have we? Are we out of touch with God?

Not at all. There is a provision in the plan of God for just such an emergency; an alternate design for sustaining communication with God in the event of a failure on our part . . .

Stand-by prayer.

In this, the Triune God automatically takes over, and performs in our stead the moment we fail to function.

The Holy Spirit, as the Spirit of Prayer, comes to our aid by pleading in our behalf with groans that words cannot express.

God the Father, Who searches our hearts, understands the mind of the Spirit, because He makes intercession for the saints in accordance with God's will.

God the Son, Who is at the right hand of the Father, intercedes for us as well, and saves us to the uttermost.

Praise God! Such is the sufficiency of grace.

God's strength is so perfected in weakness, that even when we fail to pray intelligently and can only "cry with our whole heart" . . . our prayer life continues *without interruption.*

THE FRIEND OF THE DOWNCAST

"I cried unto thee; save me, and I shall keep thy testimonies" (Psalm 119:146).

If a man is downcast . . .

If his soul continually melts for heaviness, if massive heartbreak has left him saddened beyond measure, if a long-sustained minor note pedal-points the theme of his life . . .

Where can he go with the voice of his weeping?

To a friend, perhaps . . .

If he has a friend who has gone before him on the lonely road of sorrow, and will understand his feelings as well as his words. A friend who is acquainted with grief . . . *and will not sing songs to his heavy heart, or run roughshod over his bleeding emotions, or despise him if his inner pool of tears spills over.*

To a friend, perhaps . . .

If he has a friend who will be sensitive to his silences, his disconnected outbursts, his ramblings. A friend who will hear him out . . . *and not interrupt with "that reminds me of," or cut him short with a prematurely superimposed "I know just how you feel," or turn him*

54

off with "what you should do is," or render him speechless with pointed stories of how much better others are at handling similar situations.

Where can he go with the voice of his weeping?

To a friend, perhaps . . .
If he has a friend who will accept him as he is . . . faulty, inconsistent, ambivalent. A friend who will be patient with his humanity . . . *and not label, or judge, or condemn or reject him; or take over and play Freud to his painful depression.*

To a friend, perhaps . . .
If he has a friend who is able to enter into his suffering *without falling into the pit with him,* to handle his broken heart *without wounding it further,* and to help him renew his commitment to life *without attempting to do it for him.*

To a friend, perhaps . . .
If he has a friend who is worthy of trust, *and will not betray his confidence* . . .
A friend who is available at all times, *and will not give up on him.*

And if he has such a friend as this, His Name will surely be Jesus . . .
For Jesus is the Friend of the downcast in soul.

A MERE TENDRIL OF FAITH

"I prevented the dawning of the morning, and cried; I hoped in thy word" (Psalm 119:147).

A mere tendril of faith linked Mary Magdalene to the garden sepulchre . . .

Not a faith that saw the whole picture of the resurrection, nor a faith that walked confidently in the light. But only a faith that drew close *while it was yet dark.*

She stood weeping beside the open tomb of her expectations. Emptied of hope, yet hoping against hope.

Then Jesus met her faith with a single word
And she walked in light!

So it is with us . . .

At times, our tears may rise before the dawning of the morning, but whenever our faith draws near while it is still dark . . .

We also will see the Lord.

COUNTING THOUGHTS

"Mine eyes prevent the night watches, that I might meditate in thy word" (Psalms 119:148).

In the night watches, when sleep comes slowly, let us not "count sheep . . ."

Instead, let us "count" the loving thoughts of the *Good Shepherd of the sheep:*

Fear not, little flock; for it is your Father's good pleasure to give you the kingdom.

Let not your heart be troubled, neither let it be afraid:

I am with thee, and in thee . . .

Abide in Me.

Be still
And know that I am God.

My thoughts are not your thoughts, neither are your ways my ways: for as the heavens are higher than the earth, so are my ways higher than your ways, and my thoughts than your thoughts.

What I do thou knowest not now, but I have prayed
for thee, that thy faith fail not . . .
Only believe.

I am the Good Shepherd
I will never leave thee, nor forsake thee.

When thou passest through the waters, I will be with
thee; and through the rivers, they shall not overflow
thee:
When thou walkest through the fire, thou shalt not
be burned; neither shall the flame kindle upon thee.
I am thy shield and thy exceeding great reward . . .
Come unto Me, and I will give you rest.

I am the Good Shepherd and know my sheep.
I know the thoughts that I think toward you:
thoughts of peace, and not of evil . . .
Believest thou this?

Yea, Lord, I believe.
How precious are thy thoughts unto me, O God!
How great is the sum of them . . . if I should count
them, they are more in number than the sand.

I will both lay me down in peace and sleep:
For Thou, Lord, only makest me dwell in safety.

AN AUDIENCE WITH GOD

"Hear my voice according unto thy lovingkindness: O LORD, quicken me according to thy judgments" (Psalm 119:149).

"O that someone would hear me . . ."

Such is the cry of our hearts, for God has created within us a longing to be heard and understood by our fellow man. Not only so, there is something deep within our being that yearns for an audience with God as well.

Thus our fervent pleas heavenward are often voiced in the psalms: "Consider and hear me, O Lord my God! Give ear unto my prayer, that goeth not out of feigned lips! Attend unto my cry!

"Hear my voice according unto thy loving kindness."

In His humanity, Jesus shared this feeling of need. When He was on earth, He continually *sought and found* the listening ear of God in prayer: "Father, I thank thee that thou hast heard me, and I knew that thou hearest me always."

Yet when He went to the cross, He cried in vain!

*"My God, my God, why hast thou forsaken me?
Why art thou so far from helping me, and from the
words of my roaring?*

*"O my God, I cry in the daytime, but thou hearest
not; and in the night season, and am not silent.*

"But thou art holy . . . ."

Surely, the essence of His cry is an insight into the
everlasting torment of hell. *O that Someone would
hear me!*

For to cry and not be heard, to plead for help and not
be answered, to stretch out in agonizing prayer and not
reach God . . .

Of such are the wages of sin.

None of the redeemed will ever know the loneliness
of soul Christ suffered on the cross when our iniquity
separated Him from God the Father, and our sin hid
His face that He would not hear.

We know only that because of the finished work of
Christ, we do not cry in vain. *Someone hears us!* We
have an audience with God, for we are accepted *in
Christ.*

Therefore, let us come boldly unto the throne of
grace . . .

*"O LORD, hear my voice according to thy loving-
kindness"*

MORE THAN A CONQUEROR

"They draw nigh that follow after mischief: they are far from thy law" (Psalm 119:150).

"Mommy, Mommy! Butch is after me!"

A little boy sobs and flings himself into his mother's arms. At last he is safe from the mischievous Butch. Safe from his threats, his pranks, his bullying ways.

September comes . . . and the little boy goes to school. Kindergarten, first grade, second. Then he makes a decision. In simple childlike faith, he receives Jesus as his Saviour.

The years go by . . . high school, part-time jobs, wheels, girls. Teenage awkwardness, rebellion, adjustments.

Then the letter arrives. "Greetings . . ."

From overseas, the young man writes home . . . of his need for insect repellent, shaving paraphernalia, a pocket-size New Testament. He writes of the enemy that is closing in . . . the ungodliness, the atrocities, the "mischief" that is beyond belief . . . and of the battle for faith.

The weeks drag on. Then early one morning he writes:

Dear Mom and Dad,

This will be my last letter. It will be delivered to you in case of my death. Believe me, this is an extremely hard letter to write. But I must face reality. I want you to *please* remember two things. I hope they will both help and comfort you.

First, I died for a cause in which I fully believe . . .

Second, when I die, I fully believe that my soul will go to heaven. I believe in God, and I know He takes care of His loved ones. So you know that I am really all right and I will see you both some day.

I want you to know that I love you all very much. You are the most wonderful family that anyone can ever ask for, and I thank God that I was so fortunate.

Please don't let this leave a bitter feeling in your hearts — for the service, or for the war. I guess it is something that will have to be done and men will have to die to do it.

I know the blow will be terrible, but I am praying that God will give you strength to accept the fact and He will console you.

I love you all so much . . .

He tucks the letter inside his Bible. The sun rises higher, the shadows shorten, his time comes.

And a man of twenty-one goes to be with his Lord. Victorious, triumphant . . .

More than a conqueror through Him that loved him.

EVEN THOUGH

"Thou art near, O LORD; and all thy commandments are truth" (Psalm 119:151).

Even though you have received Jesus as your Saviour and even though you know the reality of His indwelling presence . . . do you ever look at the circumstances of your life and wonder:
"Where is the Lord in all of this?"

The disciples might well have asked this question!
For after the feeding of the five thousand, Jesus departed into a mountain alone and they went down unto the sea. It was dark and the ship was in the midst of the sea, tossed with waves, for the wind was contrary.
But Jesus was not come to them.

Then He drew near, walking upon the sea. And His very presence struck terror to their souls.
In fear they cried out, "It is a spirit!"

Perhaps, like the disciples, we do not always recognize the Lord and His role in our darkest problems. Sometimes He seems so far away we see only a blurred shape. A hazy outline.

Then again, we may truly see Him one moment, only to lose sight of Him the next. For just as the disciples' ship was tossed about by the raging storm, giving them only an occasional glimpse of His approaching figure, so we tend to see Him in fits and starts.

Moreover, under extreme stress, our spirits often crest a high wave of faith, then suddenly dip low . . . and what vision we have left is clouded by a mist of tears.

We also wonder, "Where is the Lord in all of this?"

He is near!

He is walking on the turbulent sea of our contrary circumstances. He is hidden in the apparition of disaster that looms on the horizon of our imagination.

He is ever drawing closer in love . . .

So today, even though we may not see Him clearly, and even though we may feel no sense of His presence, if we will accept, by faith, *the fact of His presence: "Thou art near, O LORD . . ."*

We will know His answering voice in the midst of our storm:

"Be of good cheer, it is I, be not afraid."

FOUNDED FOREVER

"Concerning thy testimonies, I have known of old that thou hast founded them for ever" (Psalm 119:152).

Rose and her daughter stood hand in hand staring at the big hole in their backyard. What a horrible sight met their eyes!

Last week a new swimming pool company had dug for a family-size pool. This week the company was out of business.

The firm was bankrupt. The owner had disappeared.

As Rose and her daughter looked at the yawning pit before them, their reactions to the situation were quite different.

Rose thought of the problems ahead, moaned and crumpled her contract with the defunct company. *Rubbish!* It wasn't even worth the paper it was written on.

But her daughter giggled with delight! With the clear insight of a young child, she saw a precious truth. "Mother! Just imagine God saving us one week, and then going out of business the next!

"Wouldn't that be ridiculous?"

Have we thought that when we received Jesus as our Lord and Saviour, we were doing business with a fly-by-night outfit that was in danger of going bankrupt?

A here-today-gone-tomorrow enterprise that didn't

have sufficient resources to stand behind its commitments?

If we have, it would be well for us to realize that in salvation we are dealing with THE OLDEST ESTABLISHED FIRM IN EXISTENCE.

In fact, before the foundation of the world God went into the salvation business, and has been managing it successfully ever since. Behind His claims to save to the uttermost everyone who comes to Him through Christ, stand His integrity, power and resources.

In this context, then, the Bible is an agreement that God has drawn up and presented to man. It is a binding contract, *in writing,* of what He proposes to do regarding His relationship with mankind.

He spells out the terms so that there will be no misunderstanding of all that is involved. Everything is down *in black and white.* He invites us to read the fine print, count the cost — and do business with Him forever.

So don't be ridiculous!

The next time you discover a big hole in the backyard of your faith, and it looks as though God must have gone out of business . . .

Before you moan and crumple your contract with Him, won't you read it through again? Promises, completion bonds, fine print and all?

After all, God can't go out of business . . .

His testimonies were FOUNDED FOREVER!

ר

RESH

Psalm 119:153-160

My Affliction
My Advocate
He's Only The Carpenter, Mary's Son
Great Tenderness
A Love-Able Love
Tempered By Grief
This Is The Man
No Rewriting Needed

MY AFFLICTION

"Consider my affliction, and deliver me: for I do not forget thy law" (Psalm 119:153).

Alice edged forward in her chair. What did the evangelist mean when he said, "I have an affliction none of you have"?

She glanced at her friends, her mind tabulating their problems: divided homes, broken hearts, emotional disturbances, malignancies . . . *whatever could he mean?*

Alice listened carefully as he continued. "Yes, I have an affliction all my own. Something I have wrestled with all my life.

"My affliction is . . . *ME!"*

In our humanity, each of us has a *self* to cope with . . . a *me-myself-and-I* affliction that distinguishes us from all others. It is a split-off from God that is peculiarly ours; a "not Christ, but I" fragmentation from the fall.

So even when we are born again spiritually, we often function like multi-handicapped children. We live, *but not abundantly.*

We have eyes . . . yet we see so little of the hand of God in our lives. We have ears . . . yet seldom do we hear the still small voice of the Spirit.

Left to ourselves, we neither reckon beyond Number One; nor do we read the handwriting on the wall.

Like fantasy children, we live in an unreal world — disoriented to grace, out of contact with God and man. Laid low by guilt, paralyzed by fear.

Indeed, unless we are controlled by the Spirit, we are more than capable of bringing about our own downfall. For as descendents of Adam, we are naturally chips-off-the-old-block . . .

And programmed for *me-myself-and-I* affliction.

O that God would give us a good hard look at ourselves! Then our tongues would be loosed to pray:

"Lord, consider my affliction and deliver . . . ME!"

MY ADVOCATE

"Plead my cause, and deliver me: quicken me according to thy word (Psalm 119:154).

What does God do with the believer whose inherent *me-myself-and-I* affliction causes him to sin, and sin and sin? Does He disown Him? Turn against him? Weary of him?

Not at all. In grace, He provides a fully qualified advocate to plead his cause . . .

Jesus Christ the Righteous.

We do well to remember that THE COURT OF HEAVEN never adjourns. Day and night Satan, the Accuser of the Brethren, steps forward and presses charges against the elect.

Overt sins, ungodly attitudes, unknown errors, secret faults — all are brought before the divine bar of justice. Nothing is omitted.

Our guilt is self-evident. "Beyond a reasonable doubt."

What can we say in our own defense? Nothing! We

are not qualified to represent our case. *We have no voice in court.*

If we attempt to compile statistics of our "innocence," if we seek to sway the court with emotional outbursts, if we promise to renounce our sin, clean up our life and do better in the future . . .

We are acting in contempt of court!

No. As believers in Christ, our only recourse is to acknowledge our sin. "I am guilty. I have done thus and so . . ." We tell God the truth, the whole truth and nothing but the truth.

As we confess our sin, we find the court-appointed Attorney for the Defense, Jesus Christ the Righteous, is already pleading our cause. Referring the attention of the court to the cross, He identifies with us and our sin.

His nail-pierced hands attest the penalty exacted.

It is enough. "Case dismissed!"

The law of double jeopardy will not allow us to be subjected to a second trial for the same offense. The charges against us are dropped, Satan is put to flight . . .

And we are free.

Free to leave our sin behind, free to walk with the Lord in light . . .

And free to thank God the answer to "my affliction" is:

"My Advocate, Jesus Christ the Righteous."

HE'S ONLY THE CARPENTER, MARY'S SON

"Salvation is far from the wicked: for they seek not thy statutes" (Psalm 119:155).

Jesus came to his own country; and his disciples followed Him. And on the sabbath he began to teach in the synagogue; and many who heard him were astonished, saying, "Where did this man get all this? What is the wisdom given to him? What mighty works are wrought by his hands!

"Is not this the carpenter, the son of Mary and brother of James and Joses and Judas and Simon, and are not his sisters here with us?"

They took offense at him . . .
And he could do no mighty work there.

On that day long ago, salvation was "far from the wicked" of Nazareth. Even though Jesus was standing in their midst, offering Himself in His fulness, they were untouched by salvation . . .
And unavailable for mighty works.

It could not be otherwise, for when they rejected His previous revelation of Himself as the Messiah of scripture, they were left to fashion a "Jesus" of their own. In their unbelief, they tailor-made His measurements to fit their pattern for Him: *He's only the carpenter, Mary's son . . .*

Thus they cut Him down to size, and limited His working in their lives.

The pitiful thing was that they were partially right. He was a carpenter. He was Mary's Son. In His humanity, He humbled Himself and lived as a Man among men.

But He was not *only* a carpenter. Nor was He *only* Mary's son. In His deity, He was their Messiah. The Son of God.

And far above all!

Even today there are many who are so close, yet so far from salvation, because they do not seek a divine Saviour in God's statutes.

They seek merely a human "Jesus." A good man, a wise teacher, a great ideal.

They *have not* salvation because they ask not. And they *ask not* because:

"He's *only* the carpenter, Mary's son."

GREAT TENDERNESS

"Great are thy tender mercies, O LORD: quicken me according to thy judgments" (Psalm 119:156).

If it were not for the tenderness of the Lord, we would well-nigh faint at His greatness.

> *"The blessed and only Potentate*
> *The King of kings, and Lord of lords*
> *To Whom be honour and power everlasting."*

Our minds would be awed by His great glory, but our hearts would draw back in fear.

We would tremble in His presence, were His majesty not clothed in meekness, and His truth unadorned by grace:

> *"Come unto Me,*
> *All ye that labour and are heavy laden,*
> *And I will give you rest."*

"Take My yoke upon you, and learn of Me;
For I am meek and lowly in heart:
And ye shall find rest unto your souls."

And so, at His bidding, we take courage to approach the throne of His grace. By faith *in His great tenderness*, we draw nigh to "the blessed and only Potentate, the King of kings and Lord of lords . . ."

And rest our souls in His everlasting arms.

A LOVE-ABLE LOVE

"Many are my persecutors and mine enemies; yet do I not decline from thy testimonies" (Psalm 119:157).

There is a love that goes beyond being lovely or lovable, even beyond loving in the earthbound sense of the word.

It is a love without peer, a love like none other . . .

A love-able love.

It is a full-of-the-Holy-Spirit love . . .
Therefore, emptied of self. Relaxed, free. Unconcerned with the impression it is making on others. Relieved of the need to feel accepted by men. Having nothing to lose, it has nothing to fear.

It is expansive . . . open-armed, all-encompassing in its embrace of the whole world. Excluding no name from its wide margins of witness, including even enemies in its greeting of "Men, brethren, and fathers . . ."

It is expendable . . . willing to give freely of itself, to spend and be spent as a living sacrifice, a poured-out libation on the altar of God.

It is strong . . . self-contained, courageous. Able to stand fast, to function in the face of opposition. Neither coming down from the cross, nor declining from the testimonies of God. Boldly piercing hardened hearts with the sword of the Spirit.
"And God spake on this wise . . ."

It is high . . . far above all vindictiveness, malice, wrath. Towering above its enemies in order to cover their sin with a blanket of forgiveness. "Lord, lay not this sin to their charge."
It is lowly . . . at peace with itself. Stripped of pride, clothed with humility. Bent as a reed before the Spirit's moving, content with the glory of God alone.
"Behold, I see the heavens opened, and the Son of man standing on the right hand of God."

It is a full-of-faith love . . . even to the end.
"Lord Jesus, receive my spirit."

And if this love, *this love-able love*, should fall into the ground and die, as a corn of wheat before a consenting Saul . . .
Even its death will bring forth much fruit.

TEMPERED BY GRIEF

"I beheld the transgressors, and was grieved; because they kept not thy word" (Psalm 119:158).

So often we have thought of Jesus as "a Man of sorrows, and acquainted with grief," and so He was. Yet He was a Man of anger, as well.

In the Gospel according to Mark, it is written:
And Jesus entered again into the synagogue; and there was a man there which had a withered hand. And the Pharisees watched Him, whether He would heal him on the sabbath day; that they might accuse Him. And He saith unto the man which had the withered hand: "Stand forth!"

And He saith unto them, "Is it lawful to do good on the sabbath days or to do evil? to save life, or to kill?"
But they held their peace. And He looked around about on them *with anger* . . .
Being grieved for the hardness of their hearts.

As our Lord confronted the Pharisees that day, He was angry . . .

Angry and vexed with their assumption that the letter of the law was to be observed rather than the spirit behind it.

Angry and distressed because of their callousness of heart; their stubbornness of mind.

Angry and sorrowful at their obstinacy.

Angry . . . yet sinless before God
For His anger was *tempered by grief!*

Oh, how foreign to most of us is this holy anger that grieves over the sinner as well as his sin. This indignation that works the righteousness of God does not come naturally to man.

Even Moses, the most gentle of men, became so angered with the children of Israel at the waters of Meribah, that he spoke unadvisedly with his lips. "Hear now, ye rebels . . ."

And it went ill with Moses for their sakes.

Moses sinned, for he beheld the transgressors with heated anger, and sought to put them in their place. *That is, beneath himself.*

But Jesus was without sin, for His anger was tempered by grief. Cooled, strengthened and shaped by godly sorrow.

So by a soul-searching question He sought to lead the Pharisees to the place of forgiveness . . .

That is, the foot of the cross.

THIS IS THE MAN

"Consider how I love thy precepts: quicken me, O LORD, according to thy lovingkindness" (Psalm 119:159).

If ever a man could say to the Lord, "Consider how I love thy precepts . . ."

The Psalmist is the man.

The law of the Lord is better unto him "than thousands of gold and silver." He loves the commandments "above gold; yea, above fine gold."

He rejoices in the Word "as one that finds great spoil."

When his enemies "draw nigh," his soul is shielded by a truth. When he is "almost consumed," he does not forget God's statutes.

He refrains his feet "from every evil way," that he might not depart from God's Word. He inclines his heart to perform it always . . .

"Even unto the end."

O how he loves the law of the Lord!
It is his meditation "all the day."

"Seven times a day" he praises God for His righteous judgments. "At midnight" he rises to give thanks again.

"In the night watches" he awakens that he might meditate upon the Word. Though his cries "prevent the dawning of the morning," he ever hopes in its eternal truths.

The testimonies are his "counselors"
The commandments his "delights."

The statutes are his "songs . . ."
In the house of his pilgrimage.

Surely, if ever a man might seek to move the hand of God by an impressive show of love for the Word of God . . .
This is the man!

Yet this is the man who humbly approaches the Throne of Grace with the sweet simplicity of a little child . . .

"Quicken me, O LORD,
according to *thy lovingkindness."*

NO REWRITING NEEDED

"Thy word is true from the beginning: and every one of thy righteous judgments endureth for ever" (Psalm 119:160).

Virginia stared at the words she had just written.

Is this what she really meant to say? Could she have put it another way? Should the ending be changed? Or perhaps the beginning?

With a sigh, she crumpled the paper and began again.

Was there no end to this rewriting?

The writer is an adventurer into the great unknown.

Equipped with a blank sheet of paper and his favorite instrument for inscribing marks on a page, he ventures to put down in black and white the intricate workings of his mind.

For days, possibly years, his brain has been preparing for this moment: receiving impressions, making observations, cataloging feelings, cross-filing memories. Now the time has come.

He takes a deep breath, surveys the broad expanse of white paper confronting him — and suddenly his mind goes blank.

Where should he begin?

Wherever, whatever — somehow he gets started, and something or other develops. Perhaps the fires of inspiration rage, and he pens everything that comes to mind — his passions outstripping his prudence.

Then again, the coals may not be kindled, and he marches stiffly through his outline — goose-stepping to the tune of a mechanical piper.

In either case, he eventually writes something. Then he looks in wide-eyed horror at the *something* he has written!

Before his unbelieving eyes parade disjointed phrases, mixed-up metaphors and hackneyed clichés. As though that were not enough, his sentences sprawl, his descriptions wander aimlessly and his characterizations fall flat.

Worst of all, the overall form of his composition is somewhat after the order of Melchizedek: without beginning or end!

What on earth was he trying to say in the first place?

How different are the ways of God!

His Book was "true from the beginning," *perfect from the very first draft,* and has never needed to be rewritten . . .

By Him or anyone else!

SCHIN

Psalm 119:161-168

A Fellowship Of Suffering
A Precious Gem
A Time To Hate
A Launching Pad For Praise
Why Jesus Held His Peace
Business As Usual
Tyranny
Spiritual Acne

A FELLOWSHIP OF SUFFERING

"Princes have persecuted me without a cause: but my heart standeth in awe of thy word" (Psalm 119:161).

Every step he took ground ungodliness into the dust. Every breath labeled Pharisaism a lie.

It was not necessary for him to shout "Look at me!" from the housetops: his very existence witnessed to the power of his Lord. He could not be ignored, explained away or covered with a cloak of religious double-talk. He was there to be reckoned with . . .

Or done away with!

His name was Lazarus. His offense was unforgivable. *He was alive!* Raised from the dead by Jesus Christ. "By reason of him, many of the Jews went away and believed . . ."

Therefore, the chief priests hated him without a cause, and consulted that they might put him to death.

Even today the same is true.

For the resurrection life is disturbing to those spiritually dead in trespasses and sins. The mere presence of one who walks in newness of life is disquieting.

It savours not of life, *but of death unto death.*

It could not be otherwise.

For the Spirit-filled believer in Christ is *visible proof* of the invisible God. He is *flesh and blood evidence* of spiritual reality.

His supernatural life must be accounted for . . .

Or done away with.

So think it not strange if the resurrection life leads to a fellowship of suffering . . .

As well as joy.

A PRECIOUS GEM

"I rejoice at thy word, as one that findeth great spoil"
(Psalm 119:162).

Tina glanced over her shoulder at the clock on the office wall. *Overtime again! Was Joe still waiting?*

With mechanical precision, she continued to stuff envelopes for mailing: 2 pamphlets, 1 form letter, fold up, fold over, insert in an envelope, stack for sealing; 2 pamphlets, 1 form letter, fold up, fold over . . . her mind wandered.

A faint smile touched her lips as she thought of Joe, and of the beautiful engagement ring on her finger. She stole a look at it . . . then her eyes widened in unbelief. *The stone was missing!* Where could it be? It was there when she showed her ring to the girls at lunch. All she had done since then was stuff envelopes.

Envelopes! Everywhere she looked she saw envelopes. Hundreds of them. Stuffed, sealed, ready to be taken to the post office.

Frantically, Tina snatched an envelope from the nearest box and pressed it between her fingers. She could feel the pamphlets, the form letter . . . but not the loose diamond! She felt again. Nothing.

She reached for another envelope, then another. Another box, then another. On and on, on and on. Finally, when she was almost ready to give up, she felt something. With trembling fingers, she tore open the envelope . . . and the precious gem rolled into her hand. With a sob of relief, Tina slumped in her chair and laid her head down on the desk. "I found it . . .
"I found it!"

Those who have lost and found a cherished verse of Scripture will understand Tina's rejoicing — for every word of God is like a precious gem set in a golden band of love.

Thus every promise of faithfulness, every pledge of fidelity, is a token of troth till Christ comes again for His Bride.

Not only so. The very essence of the Word is like that of a flawless diamond: formed of pure substance, cut and shaped without crack or fissure, perfect in design and brilliant in fire.

Moreover, the whole canon of Holy Writ is a revealer of truth! For as a diamond breaks up light into all the colors of the rainbow, so the many-faceted testimonies reflect the prismatic glory of God!

Surely, with such a precious gem in her possession, the future Bride of Christ, His Church, would never work overtime stuffing the envelopes of life . . .
Would she?

A TIME TO HATE

"I hate and abhor lying: but thy law do I love" (Psalm 119:163).

What manner of man is the Psalmist?

He is a man after God's heart. For all that God loves, he loves. And all that God hates, he hates . . . With total hatred!

He has a time to love, and a time to hate . . . *For God's laws are written on his heart.*

It would be well for us to remember that God is balanced in His person. He loves *and hates* with equal passion.

He loves light, and hates darkness. He loves righteousness, and hates iniquity. He loves truth, and hates every false way.

He loves the pure in heart, and hates a proud look, a lying tongue, hands that shed innocent blood, an heart that deviseth wicked imaginations, feet that be swift in running to mischief, a false witness that speaketh lies, and he that soweth discord among brethren.

Moreover, His wrath is revealed from heaven against all ungodliness and unrighteousness of men, who hold the truth in unrighteousness.

Let us not deceive ourselves.

Not only the Psalmist, but God also has a time to love, and a time to hate.

And if we are indifferent in the presence of evil, and do not *hate and abhor lying* . . .

It may be we do not really *love God's truth.*

A LAUNCHING PAD FOR PRAISE

"Seven times a day do I praise thee because of thy righteous judgments" (Psalm 119:164).

O Lord, I feel so sleepy this morning. So dense, so dull.

Lord, I would like to have high and lofty thoughts of You, but I just can't seem to get off the ground so early in the day. You know I can scarcely open my eyes at all, let alone lift them. But O God, "How precious are Your thoughts to me, how great is the sum of them . . ."

Lord, I praise You for this!

When I feel so groggy in the morning, I tell myself it is because I am a "night person" and cannot be expected to be at my best in the cruel light of day. How thankful I am You are a "day-and-night Person," Lord. You "neither slumber nor sleep." You are at Your best at all times!

Lord, I praise You for this!

Lord, I still feel badly about losing my temper yesterday. My humanity was really showing! And yet, thanks to You, I come to this day with a clean slate. For when I confessed my sin, You were "faithful and just to forgive me my sin, and to cleanse me from all unrighteousness . . ."

Lord, I praise You for this!

And while we're on the subject of sin, Lord, there is this matter of my recurring "me-myself-and-I" affliction that is sure to trouble me again today — my swelled head, wagging tongue, slipped halo and all. Sometimes, I can scarcely stand to live with myself! Yet You have said, "I will never leave thee, nor forsake thee."
Lord, I praise You for this!

Besides all this, Your compassions are "new every morning." Even sleepy mornings! Already your faithfulness is up and about — "upholding me with Your hand, and compassing me about with mercies."
Lord, I praise You for this!

Well, Lord — all of a sudden the day is shaping up beautifully! I feel as though I could "mount up with wings as eagles!" Or at least, "run and not be weary, and walk and not faint."
Lord, I praise You for this!

And should this day be my last on earth, I know I have nothing to fear. For surely, "goodness and mercy shall follow me all the days of my life, and I will dwell in the house of the LORD for ever."
Lord, I praise You for this!

O Lord, what *a launching pad for praise* Your righteous judgments make! Because of them my heart is warm within me, my eyes are open to Your mercies . . .
And I can lift-off the day with joy!

WHY JESUS HELD HIS PEACE

"Great peace have they which love thy law: and nothing shall offend them" (Psalm 119:165).

In the Garden of Gethsemane, Jesus was betrayed into the hands of sinners. Then all the disciples forsook Him and fled . . .

But Jesus held His peace.

The chief priests, elders and all the counsel sought false witness against Him . . .

But Jesus held His peace . . . and answered nothing.

Again the high priests asked Him and said to Him, "Art thou the Christ, the Son of the Blessed?" "I am . . ."

"He hath spoken blasphemy! He is guilty of death!"

Then did they spit in His face, and buffeted Him . . .

But Jesus held His peace.

Peter followed Him afar. And denied Him with an oath, "I do not know the man!"

But Jesus held His peace.

For envy they delivered Him to Pilate, "What shall I do with Jesus which is called Christ?" "Crucify Him!"

He had Jesus flogged, and handed Him over to be crucified.

But Jesus held His peace.

He was cut off out of the land of the living . . . and made His grave with the wicked . . . in a sepulchre that was hewn in stone.

And on the first day of the week, at evening . . .

In the upper room, the doors were shut where the disciples were assembled in fear.

But Jesus stood in the midst . . .

And held His peace out to them!
"Peace be unto you!

The peace of God is a great peace . . . tried, tested, proved. Jesus held it through the agony of Gethsemane, the ravages of Calvary, the darkness of death and the light of the resurrection . . .

So that He might offer it to us.

And today, in the upper room of your heart
Jesus stands in the midst of your fears
And holds out His great peace . . . to you!

BUSINESS AS USUAL

"LORD, I have hoped for thy salvation, and done thy commandments" (Psalm 119:166).

Peter was a realistic man.

No one could ever accuse him of living in a dream world. A flashing sword, a cock's crow, a netful of fish . . .

These were the earthly realities of his life.

Yet the night Peter was imprisoned by Herod, double-chained between two soldiers and awaiting execution in the morning; *that same night* Peter slept so soundly the angel of the LORD had to slap him on the side and awaken him . . .

In order to deliver him from prison!

Imagine! A realist asleep in prison!

What a graphic picture of faith this is. For to face the reality of death, *and go on with the business of living* is always a mark of trust.

A vote of overwhelming confidence in the Lord.

Sometimes the greatest demonstration of the existence of our faith *is not the great dramatic events of our*

lives, but in the simple everyday routine of living.
The "business as usual" activities of life.

Such activities as eating, for example.
Now eating bread is a simple thing, as simple and commonplace as sleeping. Neither is out of the ordinary.
But to take bread and give thanks to God, and to eat it as Paul did in the midst of a tempestuous storm at sea, manifests great faith . . .
For only those *who expect to live* eat for the morrow's health.

And only those whose faith is real *continue to obey God* when deliverance is not in sight.

"Lord, I have hoped for thy salvation,
and done thy commandments."

So until deliverance knocks on our door . . .
Let us take courage to trust and obey God — to eat and sleep, wash away our tears, change our apparel and go out among people. For we know that today belongs to God, and whether we see any sign of it or not . . .
He is always doing *business as usual* in our lives.

TYRANNY

"My soul hath kept thy testimonies; and I love them exceedingly" (Psalm 119:167).

Esther loved God because He first loved her. *"I delight to do thy will,"* was the pulsebeat of her life.

But one Sunday when Esther went to church, she felt ashamed of her Christian life. A missionary speaker said, "How many of you prayed for missions *as much as you should* this last week? Stand up."

On Thursday, her sick daughter had needed extra care, so Esther hadn't been able to cover all of her prayer list.

She couldn't stand, so she felt ashamed.

Then every week at Sunday School, she heard *"We should feel guilty* for having so much when other Christians have so little." After a while, Esther began to feel guilty whenever she looked at her family — at their blessings, their home, their food, their clothing.

At Christmas, she felt guilty when she bought her son a gift. And when her husband gave her a lovely necklace, she felt so guilty she returned it to the store for credit. A few days later, she felt guilty when she spent money on a holiday luncheon with friends — so she resolved to stop going out in the coming new year.

By spring, she felt guilty about everything! Or if she didn't feel guilty, she felt guilty for not feeling guilty.

There must be something she had overlooked!

One night at prayer meeting, she tried to share her burdens with her friends (for some reason, everything was going wrong at home). "But Esther, a Christian *should always be victorious!"* said one friend. Another gave her a tract on being right with God. Then Esther felt ashamed, guilty and afraid!

Could it be that she really wasn't right with God?

At Bible Class she heard, *"You should live a radiant, overcoming Christian life.* If you aren't victorious, you're a disgrace to Christ. Don't let anyone know you're a Christian!"

Esther knew she wasn't *all she should be*, so she stopped witnessing. She stopped serving the Lord. She stopped smiling . . . and she almost stopped living.

But somehow she didn't stop *loving the Word of God.*

And in time, she came to marvel at what she had known and forgotten: she didn't have to measure up to man's tyrannical "should" in order to please God.

She had only to "keep His testimonies, and love them exceedingly."

God Himself would make her what she should be.

SPIRITUAL ACNE

"I have kept thy precepts and thy testimonies: for all my ways are before thee" (Psalm 119:168).

"Oh Mother, look at me now!"

Marilyn fairly glowed with happiness. There was a fresh look about her. A naturalness, a sense of poise.

Only a few weeks before, teen-age Marilyn had made a decision. A difficult decision that gave promise of coming maturity.

Finally facing her lack of ability to hide a bad case of skin acne, she had asked for professional help.

"Mother, that was the hardest thing I ever did. To lie under that bright light before a doctor — with all my sores uncovered!"

But now, responding to her physicians' detailed instructions for a clear complexion, Marilyn was growing in self-respect.

"Mother, look at me now. I can face people . . .

"I don't need to cover up any more!"

As believers in Christ, we often suffer with another form of acne: *spiritual acne.* The surface of our life is broken out time and again because of our lack of inner maturity.

Just when we want to appear our best, impurities in our system erupt in a most embarrassing manner. Blackheads of bitterness ooze unexpectedly . . .

And infection spreads.

Then like a teen-age girl with a bad case of acne, we can't keep our hands off! We spend hours before the mirror of "self," squeezing our pimples and picking at our sores.

But it only makes matters worse.

So we pencil-in white areas of good behaviour, hoping to cover our blemishes. Finding this is not enough, we apply protective layers of superficiality, powder with self-deceit . . .

And forget that *all our ways* are before the Lord.

When will we grow up?

When will we stop trying to treat our spiritual acne ourselves, and voluntarily uncover our sores before the Great Physician?

When will we follow His prescriptions in the Word and be healed?

When we do, we will be like Marilyn . . .
We won't need to cover up any more either!

TAU

Psalm 119:169-176

In The Citadel Of Prayer
A Man Of Few Words
"Can You Hear Me?"
Only In Love
The Scars Of Love
Homesick For Heaven
Perfected Praise
The Paths Of Righteousness

IN THE CITADEL OF PRAYER

"Let my cry come near before thee, O LORD: give me understanding according to thy word" (Psalm 119:169).

The burden of Habakkuk was heavy.

Judah, his beloved country, was living in open sin. Idolatrous loves flouted the holiness of God. Injustice, oppression and violence polluted the land. Anarchy reigned.

On the horizon loomed Chaldea, that fierce and impetuous nation. That proud heathen empire, even more wicked than Judah. Cruel, swift, heartless . . . gobbling up lesser nations with insatiable greed.

Invasion was imminent. Hope of deliverance, gone.

Habakkuk was utterly shaken. Bewildered. Questions, doubts, fears — all struggled for supremacy within his anguished soul.

Where was God in all of this? Why was He silent? Why would He use a godless nation to judge His people Israel?

If God is of purer eyes than to behold evil, and can not look on iniquity; why would He look upon them that deal treacherously, and hold His tongue when the

106

wicked devoureth the man that is more righteous than he?

"O Lord, how long shall I cry, and Thou wilt not hear! even cry out unto Thee of violence, and Thou wilt not save!"

Habakkuk looked up . . .
And his heart trembled with awe.

> *"But the Lord is in His holy temple:*
> *let all the earth keep silence before Him."*

Then God spoke . . .
And Habakkuk listened.

In the day Habakkuk prayed, God answered him, and strengthened him with strength in his soul.
Thus he was able to go on.

"Although the fig tree shall not blossom, neither shall fruit be in the vines; the labour of the olive shall fail, and the fields shall yield no meat; the flock shall be cut off from the fold, and there shall be no herd in the stalls . . .

"Yet I will rejoice in the LORD, I will joy in the God of my salvation."

Such is the victory of The Citadel of Prayer.

A MAN OF FEW WORDS

"Let my supplication come before thee: deliver me according to thy word" (Psalm 119:170).

When the Psalmist supplicates the Lord for deliverance, he is a man of few words.

He doesn't use vain repetitions
Thinking he shall be heard for much speaking.

He doesn't wander in a polysyllabled maze
Stringing daisy-chain clichés.

He doesn't stumble over the protocol of prayer
Or "thee-thou" himself into a corner.

He doesn't seek to impress God
Or instruct Him in the way He should go.

He doesn't try to move God's hand with histrionics
Or melt His heart with fevered pleas.

Rather, his prayer of supplication is a simple orientation to grace.

"Deliver me according to . . . *thy word.*"

Refreshing, isn't it?

"CAN YOU HEAR ME?"

"My lips shall utter praise, when thou hast taught me thy statutes" (Psalm 119:171).

"Joey, can you hear me? Can you hear me?"
The teacher waits until Joey's eyes are watching her lips.

"Can you hear me? This is a ball. Isn't it a pretty ball?"
As Joey comes closer, she smiles and places the ball in his hands. "Feel the ball, Joey. The ball is soft. The ball is round." Her fingers guide his as they trace the outline of the ball together. Once more she holds the ball near her lips:
"This is a ball . . . ball . . . ball."

Suddenly, the teacher drops the ball and it bounces back. Joey squeals with delight! What is the name of this fascinating object? His eyes watch her lips carefully. "Joey, can you hear me? This is a ball."
"B . . . b . . . baa," his lips move cautiously.
She holds his hand along her throat that he may feel the sound of the word. "Ball, ball, ball."

Now his jaw drops a little lower.
"B . . . baw . . . baww . . ." The final "l" sets his

tongue in motion. "Baw . . . l, bawl, ball!"

Their eyes meet in triumph! Joey can communicate at last. He can "hear" with his eyes; share thoughts with his mind. Now that he can speak understandable words with his lips, he need never again be isolated in the silent world of the totally deaf.

Contact has been made. *"Ball! Ball! Ball!"*

What is ahead for Joey? A new world! A world of wonderful words! Words to imitate, words to absorb, words to share with others. Words to associate with things around him, to express his inner feelings, to set his thoughts astir when he is taught to read and write.

Above all, words with which to offer thanks to a patient teacher who knelt to his level, and began quietly:

"Joey, can you hear me? This is a . . . *ball.*"

In like manner, the Holy Spirit ministers to our spiritual deafness. He bends over us in love, lifts before our eyes a vision of the cross of Christ, holds us close that we may feel the sound of His words and speaks in a still small voice:

"Can you hear Me? *This is love . . . love . . . love . . .*"

If we turn away, we will not hear His words — the deaf cannot hear when their back is turned. But if we truly hear His words, a whole new world awaits us. Our tongue will be loosed, and our lips will begin to utter praise . . .

With the wonderful words He has taught us.

ONLY IN LOVE

"My tongue shall speak of thy word: for all thy commandments are righteousness" (Psalm 119:172).

There is a ministry that God has extended to each one of His children. It is at once a precious privilege . . .
And an awesome responsibility.

It is the ministry of speaking the Word of God to others on a one-to-one, person-to-person basis.
Of speaking the truth. *Only the truth.*
And speaking it in love.
Only in love.

For the word of God is the expression of His love.
It meets us where we are in our humanity and communicates the redemptive love of a holy God through commandments, promises and exhortations.
It cannot be divorced from love . . .
For it was given in love.

Therefore, if we give the truth to another without giving him love, if we remove the divine content of

112

compassion and speak words only . . .

If we "hurl volleys of scripture texts at backsliders, and launch sermons at the broken-hearted before their bleeding wounds are stanched . . ."

We distort the Word of God.

For God speaks the truth. *Only the truth.*
And He speaks it in love.
Only in love.

THE SCARS OF LOVE

"Let thine hand help me; for I have chosen thy precepts" (Psalm 119:173).

To love is to be vulnerable.

To love without defense is to be wide open for whatever comes. It is to be without protection. Uncovered. Unguarded.

The more one loves in this way, the more deeply he may be hurt by the one whom he loves. For to that one, as to no one else, the inner recesses of the heart are exposed.

Therefore, *the heart that loves* may well be wounded.

Only when there has been a wound can there be any concept of the depth of the love. A shallow love will shrink when it feels the slightest pain, but a deep love will absorb piercing blows, revealing a richness that could not otherwise be brought to light.

The wideness of the love is revealed as well. If the opening to one's heart is narrowed as a result of being hurt, the dimensions of the love have also been defined.

It goes thus far, *but no farther.*
It includes this, *but not that.*

Conversely, if the heart that was wounded still loves as openly as before, the very presence of the scars testify to the breadth of the love.
It goes beyond that which hurt it.
Far, far beyond.

Thus the scars are a written guarantee
Of the reality of the love.

"O LORD, let thine hand help me . . ."

HOMESICK FOR HEAVEN

"I have longed for thy salvation, O LORD; and thy law is my delight" (Psalm 119:174).

O Lord . . .
Even the sparrow has found a home and the swallow a nest, but my soul is restless.
My soul longs, yes, is homesick for heaven.

But how can this be?
How can I be homesick for a place I have never known?

O Lord, I wonder . . .
Yesterday morning a soft breeze tumble-dried the rain-washed air. And in the late afternoon, as I stood high on the crest of a hill, I looked down on my still-sparkling valley.
Could anything be more beautiful?

Then I looked into the valley beyond, and caught my breath!

All was gold!
Yellow gold, bronze gold, apricot, tangerine
Sun, earth, clouds, trees, grass, distant sea
Glowing, shimmering, pulsating gold.

It was as though the glory of heaven had broken through the bondage of corruption, and bathed all it touched with transcendent light. As though for a moment the curse had been lifted, the curtain drawn . . .

And I saw the earth redeemed!

Lord, I think this is it . . .
A figure of the true.

For I am as the earth. I also groan within myself waiting for the fulness of my salvation.
I see through a glass darkly.

Yet, even now there are moments when the gentle breeze of Your Spirit blows aside the smog of my humanity, and I know in part.

And there have been a few golden hours, I could count them on the fingers of one hand, when I have looked into the life beyond and had a foretaste of heaven.

O Lord, who can wait?

Even the sparrow has found a home and the swallow a nest, but my soul is increasingly restless.

My soul longs, yes, is homesick for heaven.

PERFECTED PRAISE

"Let my soul live, and it shall praise thee; and let thy judgments help me" (Psalm 119:175).

Praise is precious to the Lord . . .

When Jesus went into the temple of God, the little children cried out their praise. And He was pleased!
"Out of the mouth of babes and sucklings thou has perfected praise!"

If the simplicity of their praise was so acceptable to Him, will he not also perfect the praise of His "older" children?
Will He not treasure the praise that has been tested over the years in the furnace of affliction?
Is it not pure gold?

The older we grow, the more we may become *living testimonies of praise* to the Lord. Our very lives are evidence of His sustaining grace. His deliverances have obviously been greater than our battles!

"I have been young, and now am old; yet have I not seen the righteous forsaken."

Surely, this is cause for praise!

Looking back over the years, we see that every testing has had its "way of escape"; every valley its "green pastures." He has always brought us through.

"There failed not ought of any good thing which the Lord had spoken . . . all came to pass."

Shall we not also praise Him for this?

In our confession, He has forgiven us
In our confusion, He has guided us
In our falling, He has upheld us with His hand
In our loneliness, He has assured us with His presence.

In our sorrow, He has had compassion on us
In our weakness, He has strengthened us
In all our sickness, He has let our soul live . . .
That we may praise Him!

Truly, praise is most precious to the Lord.

And a praise that has been perfected through testing is an acceptable *and accepted* offering . . .

Pure gold in His sight.

THE PATHS OF RIGHTEOUSNESS

"I have gone astray like a lost sheep; seek thy servant; for I do not forget thy commandments" (Psalm 119:176).

Once there was a young lamb who followed his Shepherd with a whole heart. He walked with Him in THE PATHS OF RIGHTEOUSNESS.

His Shepherd preserved him withersoever he went, and gave him many green pastures . . .

And would have given more.

One day the Shepherd's flock journeyed to a dangerous land: THE VALLEY OF THE SHADOW OF DEATH. But this lamb (who was older now) sent other lambs in his place . . .

And he laid down to rest.

At eventide, when he arose, he walked alone upon the high places of his pleasant land. His eyes wandered past his own boundaries and into another sheep's pasture. It was greener than his own.

There he saw a lamb bathing beside the waters. A little ewe lamb. She was very beautiful to look upon. He paused . . .

And his desires went out to her.

Suddenly, he despised the commandment of his Shepherd, and left THE PATHS OF RIGHTEOUS-NESS. He wallowed in THE MUD OF DEFILE-MENT, and gave great occasion for the enemies of his Shepherd to blaspheme. He delighted himself with the little ewe lamb . . .

And caused her master to be put to death.

Gone astray like a lost sheep
Unable to find his way back
Hiding from his Shepherd . . .

He knew no rest
Until he acknowledged his transgression.

According to His lovingkindness, the Shepherd of the sheep had mercy upon him. According to the multitude of His tender mercies, He blotted out his iniquities, and created within him a clean heart.

In steadfast love, He washed him whiter than snow, and anointed his head with oil. He restored his soul . . .

And the joy of his salvation.

Once more the lamb followed his Shepherd with a whole heart. He gladly walked in THE PATHS OF RIGHTEOUSNESS for His Name's sake.

Goodness and mercy followed him all the days of his life . . .

And he shall dwell in THE HOUSE OF THE LORD for ever.

(2 Samuel 11, 12:1-25; Psa. 51; Psa. 23)